CULTURE of INQUIRY

Healthy Debate in the Boardroom

by Nancy R. Axelrod

D1567594

BOARDSOURCE®
Building Effective Nonprofit Boards

Library of Congress Cataloging-in-Publication Data

Axelrod, Nancy R.

Culture of inquiry : healthy debate in the boardroom / by Nancy R. Axelrod.
    p. cm.

ISBN 1-58686-103-4 (pbk.)

1. Nonprofit organizations—Management.   2. Boards of directors.   3. Communication in organizations.   4. Discussion.   I. BoardSource (Organization) II. Title.   III. Title: Debate in the boardroom.

HD62.6.A936 2007

658.4'22—dc22

                    2007023740

Published by BoardSource
1828 L Street, NW, Suite 900
Washington, DC 20036

BOARDSOURCE®
Building Effective Nonprofit Boards

BoardSource, formerly the National Center for Nonprofit Boards, is the premier resource for practical information, tools and best practices, training, and leadership development for board members of nonprofit organizations worldwide. Through our highly acclaimed programs and services, BoardSource enables organizations to fulfill their missions by helping build strong and effective nonprofit boards.

BoardSource provides assistance and resources to nonprofit leaders through workshops, training, and our extensive Web site, www.boardsource.org. A team of BoardSource governance consultants works directly with nonprofit leaders to design specialized solutions to meet organizations' needs and assists nongovernmental organizations around the world through partnerships and capacity building. As the world's largest, most comprehensive publisher of materials on nonprofit governance, BoardSource offers a wide selection of books, videotapes, CDs, and online tools. BoardSource also hosts the BoardSource Leadership Forum, bringing together governance experts, board members, and chief executives of nonprofit organizations from around the world.

Created out of the nonprofit sector's critical need for governance guidance and expertise, BoardSource is a 501(c)(3) nonprofit organization that has provided practical solutions to nonprofit organizations of all sizes in diverse communities. In 2001, BoardSource changed its name from the National Center for Nonprofit Boards to better reflect its mission. Today, BoardSource has approximately 11,000 members and has served more than 75,000 nonprofit leaders.

For more information, please visit our Web site, www.boardsource.org, e-mail us at mail@boardsource.org, or call us at 800-883-6262.

Have You Used These BoardSource Resources?

VIDEOS

Meeting the Challenge: An Orientation to Nonprofit Board Service

Speaking of Money: A Guide to Fundraising for Nonprofit Board Members

BOOKS

The Board Chair Handbook

Managing Conflicts of Interest: A Primer for Nonprofit Boards

Driving Strategic Planning: A Nonprofit Executive's Guide

Taming the Troublesome Board Member

The Nonprofit Dashboard: A Tool for Tracking Progress

Presenting: Nonprofit Financials

Meet Smarter: A Guide to Better Nonprofit Board Meetings

The Nonprofit Policy Sampler, Second Edition

Getting the Best from Your Board: An Executive's Guide to a Successful Partnership

The Nonprofit Board Answer Book — A Practical Guide for Board Members and Chief Executives, Second Edition

The Source: Twelve Principles of Governance That Power Exceptional Boards

The Nonprofit Legal Landscape

Self-Assessment for Nonprofit Governing Boards

Assessment of the Chief Executive

Fearless Fundraising

The Nonprofit Board's Guide to Bylaws

Understanding Nonprofit Financial Statements

Transforming Board Structure: Strategies for Committees and Task Forces

The Board Building Cycle: Nine Steps to Finding, Recruiting, and Engaging Nonprofit Board Members, Second Edition

THE GOVERNANCE SERIES

1. *Ten Basic Responsibilities of Nonprofit Boards*
2. *Financial Responsibilities of Nonprofit Boards*
3. *Structures and Practices of Nonprofit Boards*
4. *Fundraising Responsibilities of Nonprofit Boards*
5. *Legal Responsibilities of Nonprofit Boards*
6. *The Nonprofit Board's Role in Setting and Advancing the Mission*
7. *The Nonprofit Board's Role in Planning and Evaluation*
8. *How To Help Your Board Govern More and Manage Less*
9. *Leadership Roles in Nonprofit Governance*

For an up-to-date list of publications and information about current prices, membership, and other services, please call BoardSource at 800-883-6262 or visit our Web site at www.boardsource.org.

Contents

How To Use This Book

It's hard to argue with Benjamin Franklin's proposition that "the good particular men may do separately...is small, compared with what they may do collectively." Any group will make better decisions if its individual members draw information from multiple sources, tap into their peers' collective expertise, and focus on the best interests of the organization. The collective wisdom of nonprofit boards is their greatest asset. But a high-performing team learns what it takes to convert that wisdom into value not through osmosis, but through conscious practices.

Certain competencies characterize boards that make a collective difference. *The Source: Twelve Principles of Governance That Power Exceptional Boards* (BoardSource, 2005) identifies a set of qualities that distinguish exceptional boards from their merely responsible, mediocre, or dysfunctional counterparts. One of these principles is a culture of inquiry — a boardroom climate that fully enlists multiple skills, differences of opinion, and informed questions. The results of this mode of governing are a board that engages and energizes its members, uses meeting time productively, owns and supports its choices, and ultimately makes better decisions. By leveraging its collective wisdom, a board with a culture of inquiry advances the mission of the organization. Without a culture of inquiry, the same board can risk groupthink, inertia, disengagement, and poor decision making.

But how does a board develop a culture of inquiry? I believe that it cannot do so unless four building blocks are in place: trust, information sharing, teamwork, and dialogue. The majority of the material in this book focuses on these building blocks; the beginning two chapters help readers understand what a culture of inquiry is, why it is important, and how to assess whether a board already has such a culture.

Chapter 1 explains where the term culture of inquiry comes from, what it is (and is not), and why it matters to a high-functioning board. You'll learn who and what influences board culture and how board culture works, along with examples that illustrate the concept. Chapter 2 shows you how to assess your board's current culture of inquiry, discusses barriers to creating a culture of inquiry, and introduces the four essential building blocks. Subsequent chapters each focus on a particular building block, describing what each looks like in practice and providing specific strategies to help your board use the blocks to help shape behavior. Many readers will benefit from reading about these blocks in the order that they appear. Reading chapters in order can facilitate the learning experience and enhance the likelihood that you will be able to foster a culture of inquiry on your board. Other readers may jump directly to the chapter that addresses things they'd like to achieve with their boards. Either choice can be useful; select the best option for you. Chapter 3 focuses on trust, the first building block, and a foundation without which a culture of inquiry is impossible. Chapter 4 is about information sharing and offers many tools to help boards do this easily and efficiently. Chapter 5 offers tools for cultivating teamwork and addresses leadership, the role of outside experts, and regular board assessment. Chapter 6 provides tools for stimulating dialogue, with emphasis on meeting formats, ways to frame questions to encourage generative thinking, and tips for practicing constructive dissent.

Tools, of course, are only the beginning. The desire to move from being a merely responsible board to becoming an exceptional one is also necessary. I hope that, after reading this book, you and your board will decide that fostering a culture of inquiry is one way to help you better serve your organization. I can assure you that the outcome will be worth the effort.

1.

What Is a Culture of Inquiry, and Why Does It Matter?

A board's culture consists of a combination of formal and informal rules, agreements, and traditions that have developed slowly and unconsciously over time. Culture determines who makes the decisions, who speaks to whom and in what manner, how board and staff members relate to each other, and even where board members sit at the board table. Culture also drives decisions about what role the chief executive has in board meetings, where the board invests the lion's share of its time, and what issues are considered sacred cows. Although the norms that make up a board's culture can be hard to pin down, they have a significant influence on the ways board members work together and engage with management to carry out the board's work.

Nonprofit leaders have different perceptions about what the board's norms should be. And they don't always believe a culture of inquiry is the optimal choice. There may be a disconnect in some corners between the strategic leadership role the field now tells us that nonprofit boards should play and the expectations that some nonprofit leaders have for their boards. For some organizations, desirable board cultures simply reward the board for staying out of operations or minimizing dissent. For others, an effective culture limits the board's work to fulfilling its fiduciary obligations and reacting to management's recommendations. Individuals who prefer control, the appearance of continuous harmony in board deliberations, or quick decision making are not likely to be chief proponents of a culture of inquiry.

Moreover, the notion of a "heroic ideal" board may not be on every chief executive's radar screen, as this quote (from a report on projected executive leadership transitions in the nonprofit sector) reveals: "For the most part I have always accepted that my job [as executive director] was to do the work of the board, to prepare everything for them, to make sure they had what they needed to do the fiduciary job, to give them communication, to control the message. Now the board experts are telling me that the board really needs to assume much more responsibility and ownership."[1]

HOW CULTURE BECOMES A CULTURE OF INQUIRY

The norms that characterize a culture of inquiry include

- a sense of mutual respect, trust, and inclusiveness among board members

- the capacity to explore divergent views in a respectful rather than adversarial manner

---

1. Quoted in Jeanne Bell, Richard Moyers, and Timothy Wolfred, *Daring to Lead 2006: A National Study of Nonprofit Executive Leadership* (CompassPoint and Meyer Foundation, 2006). www.compasspoint.org/daringtolead2006

Basic Board Roles

A culture of inquiry supports the fundamental governance roles of a nonprofit board. Governance consultant Berit M. Lakey says the traditional notion of the board as policy maker is too limited. She describes three major roles, each with specific responsibilities:

1. Setting organizational direction

   Strategic planning

   Operational or annual planning

2. Ensuring the necessary resources

   Capable staff leadership

   Adequate financial resources

   Positive public image

3. Providing oversight

   Financial oversight

   Risk management

   Program monitoring and evaluation

   Legal and moral oversight

   Evaluation of the chief executive

   Board self-assessment

Source: Berit M. Lakey, *Nonprofit Governance: Steering Your Organization with Authority and Accountability* (Washington, DC: BoardSource, 2000).

- a willingness to gather relevant information to inform decisions

- equal access to information

- the presence of active feedback mechanisms that help the board engage in continuous improvement and

- an individual and collective commitment to decisions, plans of action, and accountability to follow through on the board's agreements

Boards that foster a culture of inquiry are not afraid to question complex, controversial, or ambiguous matters or look at issues from all sides. A healthy culture of inquiry promotes thoughtful decision making, even when the decisions are tough ones. When dialogue, candor, and dissent are all part of group dynamics, board members master the skills of listening, dissecting the issues, and responding thoughtfully, truthfully, and in the best interests of the organization. Learning and information gathering are important ingredients in a culture of inquiry, since decision making and accountability depend on board members' confidence that they are knowledgeable about various sides of an issue. Furthermore, board members in a culture of inquiry don't accept easy answers. Vigilance is part of the culture, and board members are aware that difficult questions need deliberation, and that situations that seem trouble-free may encompass deeper, more complicated issues.

Over the last few years, well-publicized scandals and allegations of improper practices have weakened public trust and heightened scrutiny of both nonprofit and for-profit organizations. A growing number of nonprofit organizations are complying voluntarily with some of the provisions in the Sarbanes-Oxley Act of 2002, which imposes rigorous financial, management, and governance controls primarily on publicly traded corporations. A healthy culture of inquiry can do much to advance the responsible self-regulation and proactive governance the public expects of nonprofit leaders.

WHAT A CULTURE OF INQUIRY IS NOT

Governing in a culture of inquiry does not mean encouraging board members to meddle, dispute, or endlessly question every issue or recommendation brought to the board. After all, decisions must be made in real time, and board members are mostly volunteers with busy day jobs who come together for limited periods. Board chairs, chief executives, and board committee chairs can determine which issues warrant a closer look. They can also be good arbiters of when to move from intelligence gathering and inquiry to debate and action.

A culture of inquiry is not a culture of indecision. The amount of time a board spends deliberating on each agenda item is not a metric for gauging a culture of inquiry. Many matters and decisions require approval but not necessarily inquiry or discussion. A board that takes inquiry to an illogical extreme by deferring action until every single viewpoint or option is fully vetted could create a culture of indecision and avoidance. For example, approving the minutes from the last board meeting is more likely to require a relatively perfunctory board action than a decision to use a portion of the reserve fund to finance an unexpected threat or to support a new venture.

Ram Charan describes a familiar scenario of employees reluctant to challenge a chief executive, a scenario that is relevant to boards. He believes leaders must be responsible for changing the climate: "Breaking a culture of indecision requires a leader who can engender intellectual honesty and trust in the connections between people. By using each encounter with his or her employees as an opportunity to model open, honest, and decisive dialogue, the leader sets the tone for the entire organization."[2] Charan emphasizes the importance of open dialogue at all levels as the foundation of a culture of decisive behavior, which is compatible with a culture of inquiry. Granted, achieving this ideal is easier said than done when there are so many well-publicized examples of imperial chief executives who discouraged or penalized board and staff members for attempting to penetrate their thick layer of hubris.

---

2. Ram Charan, "Conquering a Culture of Indecision," *Harvard Business Review*, April 2001.

WHO AND WHAT INFLUENCE A CULTURE OF INQUIRY

Board culture is hard to measure in ways that satisfy social science standards. My three decades of experience as a board anthropologist have taught me that it is an ongoing challenge for most boards to establish a strong, positive culture that transcends (if not survives) any individual or group of individuals. Like all cultures, a board's norms of behavior are passed from one generation of members to the next. Certain practices become so deeply ingrained in group behavior that they occur almost without anyone being conscious of them.

Bruno Bettelheim, the eminent child psychologist, was often asked for his advice on how to be a good parent. His response: "It depends on what kind of a child you want to have." So it goes for boards. The kind of board the organization wants to have will be defined either explicitly or implicitly by its leaders, especially the board chair and the chief executive (and other board officers). A culture of inquiry flourishes when its principles and practices are congruent with the values of the leaders who keep the flame.

THE BOARD CHAIR AND THE CHIEF EXECUTIVE

The board chair who can question others without alienating them and knows how to learn and listen authentically will be a good role model in a culture of inquiry. A different culture is likely to result when the chair imposes ideological rigidity or is afraid to invite views that don't mesh with those of the majority. The best board chairs have two essential capabilities: guiding the board without overpowering it and building consensus without inhibiting debate on issues that do not lend themselves to easy solutions.

If the chief executive sees the board as an asset and a partner in pursuing the organization's mission and goals, then he or she is more likely to promote a culture of inquiry. But if the chief executive views the board as a necessary nuisance, he or she is less likely to invite the board to weigh in genuinely on strategic issues that matter. While chief executives who view the board as governance partners welcome differing points of view and strategic thinking at the board table, they also recognize their own critical role in giving the board the tools for stewardship and strategy.

ORGANIZATIONAL LIFE CYCLE

A board's culture is also influenced by the organization's developmental stage or unique conditions. For example, the members of a founding board of a new organization might function more as surrogate administrators than as stewards. An organization in crisis may look to a few individuals on the board to chart the course until confidence is restored or an executive leadership vacuum is filled. The board's capacity for a culture of inquiry fluctuates over time as board composition, board leadership, and needs of the organization change.

CHANGING AND SUSTAINING A CULTURE OF INQUIRY

Boards cannot easily change their cultures. Rather than seizing the governance model du jour, the board and management team need to articulate the board's role (beyond the boilerplate language in the bylaws). The board can raise its awareness of trade-offs by asking itself some hard questions. Just how much does the board want to be engaged — beyond discharging its legal duties — in matters such as envisioning direction? Should the board be invited to shape strategy or react to management's decisions? Is it realistic to capitalize on the full range of talents present on the board or better to rely on the work of a small group of board members who make decisions for the rest of the board? Will it be more helpful for the board to focus on oversight of immediate concerns or to devote more of its time to future direction? If the board can add value to tactical or operational issues, which issues warrant its time and attention at this level?

The desired board culture cannot be sustained unless a majority of board members and the staff who support the board are invited to help create and accept the conditions to make it work. It takes more than one person to change or sustain culture. These norms and attitudes must be ingrained in the way the organization does business and communicated to new board and staff members. A board's culture can be passed on by

- using board orientation to introduce the board's rules of engagement and its primary domains of work

- sharing organizational stories with new board members

- mentoring new board members throughout their first year on the board

- observing the behavior of longer-serving board members who serve as role models

- making sure board members have firsthand experience with programs and services

- giving board and staff opportunities to get to know one another

THE MGM MANDATE: ASK AT ANY COST

Dominant board members and strong chief executives can create disincentives for board members to speak up in a manner that would create discord with other board members or management. The fears of being put in a position of assigning blame, producing remedies, or bringing negative publicity to the organization — let alone losing one's position or standing in the organization — are very real. Samuel Goldwyn, the former chief executive of MGM, demonstrated this after a string of box office failures incited him to demand that his senior team tell him what was wrong with his or the company's performance. In a *Dilbert*-like addendum, he insisted on this candid feedback "even if it costs you your jobs." Unfortunately, some nonprofit board and staff members who have raised these kinds of concerns and questions have been marked as irresponsible whistleblowers, fired, or invited to move on.

TWO CULTURE ILLUSTRATIONS

Two real-world examples may help to explain a culture of inquiry: one in which its breach resulted in adverse consequences and another in which this way of working has been institutionalized as a board practice.

LESSONS NOT TO LEARN FROM ENRON

Enron is a useful illustration for nonprofit and for-profit boards alike because in spite of adherence to conventional governance benchmarks — such as the right board size, composition, committee structure, and conflict-of-interest policy — the board and executive leadership failed, and did so spectacularly. Jeffrey Sonnenfeld, associate dean of the Yale School of Management, theorizes that "at Enron, there was a pervasive group morality, fueled in part by a shared antipathy toward energy regulation and other forms of government oversight that were perceived as anachronistic. Those who questioned the company's reckless entrepreneurship and conflicts of interest were considered problematic employees lacking perspective."[3] But why did a board of smart, able people so deeply misunderstand the financial condition of the company? And why did the board not appear to ask tough, probing questions or challenge management when things did not seem to make sense?

When Sonnenfeld looked more closely at the boards of high-profile companies like Enron, WorldCom, and Tyco, he found no broad pattern of corruption or incompetence. But when he compared them with boards considered the best in the field, he did find a correlation between the board's ability to work as a group and its overall performance. Specifically, he isolated the degree to which the board was performing as a "high-functioning work group" as the most salient difference in great boards.

In Enron's case, a number of individuals understood that something was wrong. Many suppressed their concerns and questions. Others who voiced their concerns were either ignored or penalized. In an interview, former Enron Vice President Sherron Watkins concluded that "Ken Lay's failure was that he just wanted to hear good news." It is hard not to conclude from reviewing the trial coverage of those corporate chief executives of major companies (who now are most familiar to us as "defendants") that one of the hardest things in the world is to find people who will say to a successful and powerful leader that he or she may be wrong. Unfortunately, nonprofit board members have also been reluctant to challenge charismatic or successful chief executives until a problem emerges.

STANDING ASIDE FOR THE GOOD OF THE GROUP

Governance in Quaker organizations is imbued with the values and practices of the faith, such as periods of silence for deliberation and the goal of reaching consensus on decisions. At one Quaker school, many board members feel comfortable offering opposing points of view during meetings. "We cherish this and collectively feel that

---

3. J. A. Sonnenfeld, "Why it's so hard to blow the whistle," *Yale Alumni Magazine,* March/April 2005.

board members would be of little value if they could not apply their own critical thinking and offer their views," explains the school's director.

One two-day board meeting included discussion of a proposed policy to make school housing available to same-gender employee couples on the same basis as housing is made available to married heterosexual couples. The board had approved the principle of the policy at an earlier meeting but had delayed full approval until the language was revised to the board's satisfaction. A new board member was present who had missed the meeting where the policy had been introduced. This board member was a parent of a young student in the school. "She spoke from her heart," the school's director recalled, "saying that she could not join with this policy, and that it was likely to trouble some other lower-school families. Her concern was rooted in her deep Christian belief, and her concern was for other families who held similar beliefs."

The board member's statement prompted a discussion about the school's mission, rooted in the Quaker faith, and the importance of promoting the new housing policy because of Quaker beliefs in inclusiveness and diversity. The director asked the board member "if she would be willing to 'stand aside,' meaning (state) her inability to join in the policy, but not to oppose its passage as being consistent with the core values of the school. She promised to pray and sleep on it."

"The next morning we revisited the topic. Several board members paid particular attention, listening to and affirming the troubled member's concern, but the clear energy of the group was to proceed. We did, with our troubled member standing aside, and [declaring] her personal inability to unite with the decision, but her willingness to distinguish between her personal faith and view and a decision of the larger group. I and others followed up with her afterward. It is my belief that we adopted the policy without trampling on the concerns of our member, yet she clearly felt comfortable voicing a position contrary to that of just about everyone else in the room."

While most organizations don't embrace Quaker principles, this idea is applicable to any group. It's important to affirm the right of any member to disagree with the group and equally important for dissenting members to abstain from voting if they cannot do so in good faith. An abstention allows the group to go forward. This scenario is far more likely to occur when the dissenters believe in the integrity of the decision-making process.

2.

Assessing Your Board's Culture of Inquiry

How do you know whether your board has a culture of inquiry? Like the board of the Quaker school described in chapter 1, do you have an atmosphere in which board members can agree to disagree? Or are board members reluctant to challenge each other or the chief executive? The following questions will help you learn whether your board already has a culture of inquiry or needs to develop one.

If you want to introduce the idea of a culture of inquiry to your board, consider devoting time at a board meeting to the topic and inviting all board members to respond to the following kinds of questions in a survey prior to the meeting. Compile the results and share them at the meeting to give board members an opportunity to discuss what's working well and what could be working better. As you're answering these questions, think about what has transpired at board meetings during the past six months.

- How well do we foster a sense of inclusiveness among all board members?

- Do you find board members open to listening to differences of opinions with their peers or with executive leadership?

- How comfortable are board members in engaging in constructive debate within the boardroom on consequential issues about which there are clearly divergent views?

- Do board members receive materials in advance of board meetings that provide appropriate background for discussing issues or making decisions?

- Are different formats used for board meetings, such as small-group discussions, facilitated sessions on strategic issues, or outside speakers?

- Does the board enlist information from outside the organization, such as articles, research, reports, or feedback from external experts or stakeholders on issues that require additional expertise?

- Do the board and staff collaborate to determine what information the board needs to make important decisions?

- How willing are board members to ask for additional information?

- Does the board chair try to engage all board members in discussions?

- What mechanisms or habits help ensure that all voices are heard?

- Are board members acknowledged for asking great questions?

- Does the board spend sufficient time exploring the alternatives and the consequences before it makes critical decisions?

- When making or following board decisions, how do board members put the interests of the organization above all else?

- What mechanisms does the board enlist for feedback on its performance, such as meeting evaluations or board self-assessment tools?

- How effective is the board in reaching sustainable agreements on complex or controversial issues?

- What suggestions do you have for enhancing the way in which our board works together as a group?

A SENSE OF WONDER

Intellectual curiosity is a wonderful lubricant to a culture of inquiry, as long as it does not become an end in itself that defers decision making. If you are fortunate enough to recruit and retain board members who come with what Douglas Orr, the former president of Warren Wilson College, referred to as the art of wonder, don't waste this precious asset. During his 2006 commencement address (his last year as president), Dr. Orr described this Cherokee hallmark of a fulfilled life: "If we are ever to survive as a species, we must never cease wondering. A sense of wonder calls for the skills of listening and observing, or as one writer put it, 'simply paying attention.' It is the wellspring of artistic expression — music, painting, writing. And yet it also is a precursor to all educational endeavor, from the humanities to the natural sciences." While the boardroom is not a place where unlimited debate can flourish in the same manner as in academe, the ability to ask thoughtful questions is one of the most important ways that individual board members can contribute their intellectual capital and make informed decisions.

HOW TO KNOW WHEN A CULTURE OF INQUIRY IS MISSING OR COMPROMISED

A culture of inquiry is dynamic. It moves in and out of balance in response to changing leaders and events. Just as it's important to know the hallmarks of a culture of inquiry, it's helpful to be able to spot the warning flags that such a culture is absent or waning. Here are some indicators of a missing or compromised culture of inquiry, which are especially critical when they describe chronic conditions rather than occasional lapses:

- Board members continually disagree about what norms of behavior they should follow to be effective as a group.

- The most articulate speakers and the quickest thinkers typically get the most airtime.

- Board members chronically interrupt each other.

- Board members are discouraged from requesting information that informs their decisions or understanding about how the organization works, beyond what they are given by management.

- Differences of opinion are treated as conflict that needs to be either quelled or resolved.

- Board members are not comfortable questioning long-held assumptions of board or staff members in the boardroom.

- When board members question their colleagues, their questions are often delivered or perceived as personal attacks or accusations.

- Board members listen to each other primarily to rehearse what they want to say when they react rather than listen to understand differences in views.

- It is not usually clear where everyone stands on controversial issues because some board members remain quiet.

- The board does not routinely draw on the full range of experience and skills that reside within its membership.

- Board members are discouraged from gathering information from outside sources when it would inform the board's decisions on important or complex issues.

- Board members are not encouraged to generate alternative courses of action or examine the potential consequences of high-stakes decisions the board is called on to make.

- Disagreement is treated as disloyalty, and consensus is considered unanimity.

- Board members are reluctant to voice their concerns before reaching a collective decision. Once a decision is made, individual board members challenge the decision-making process or outcome — outside of rather than during the board meeting.

These indicators suggest that when members of a group are not encouraged to seek information from multiple sources and perspectives, question assumptions, and engage in constructive deliberation, it is much easier for the group to resort to other questionable decision-making modes. The group might, for example, simply let the most powerful individuals decide. It might ignore discordant data or expert advice and act largely on the basis of personal bias. It might silence divergent views to avoid conflict in order to make a quick decision.

"THE ABILENE PARADOX"

A culture of inquiry is an antidote to groupthink, which occurs when the striving for unanimity among board members trumps their motivation to realistically appraise alternative courses of action. This mindset is a particular danger when a board is highly homogenous in social background and ideology or when it isolates itself from outside experts. This can create an insular circle that becomes disdainful of disagreement and indifferent to contrary arguments.

The closer a group is, the less likely its members are to break the cohesion by questioning and challenging, as illustrated in Jerry Harvey's Abilene Paradox. Harvey tells the story about several members of a Texas family sitting around on a hot day trying to decide about driving a couple hours to Abilene for dinner because they think the others want to go. The trip is long and hot, and the food is bad. Only when they return home do they realize that no one wanted to go in the first place, but everyone said they did because they wanted to placate the others. When individual board members are not invited to express minority views, they may go to Abilene or undermine the board action after it has been taken. Neither action contributes to informed decision making.

BARRIERS TO CREATING A CULTURE OF INQUIRY

If you view your board as a strategic asset to be leveraged rather than a legal necessity to be endured, the idea of a culture of inquiry probably resonates with you, and you may want to make it part of your organization's philosophy of governance. However, a culture of inquiry will appear dissonant to board and staff members who prize certitude over ambiguity and compliance over dialogue. And if the board's culture has been conflict-averse or hierarchical, it will not be an easy transition. If the board does not have strong collective commitment from the chief executive and board chair, efforts to create or maintain a culture of inquiry are more likely to be episodic and ephemeral. But even with these two key "process champions," some board members resist because of a low tolerance for process and a high need for results.

Another reason board members may resist is that most boards prefer to spend the majority of their limited time trying to do the work they need to do and less time examining how the board itself operates. Not enough boards periodically ask themselves how well they are doing. While some board members may scoff at any attempts at self-reflection, believing that it distracts the board from real work to be done, investing in building a healthy culture of inquiry can save time in the long run. When better discussions lead to better decisions, the board's time is used more effectively and efficiently to advance both the board and the organization.

A culture of inquiry may also be constrained by board members' perceptions that they lack experience and understanding. Some board members may struggle to ask hard questions because they feel they don't understand the intricacies of the organization's work as well as the chief executive does. They are reluctant to offer their own ideas because they fear these are not important or previous board or staff members would have already thought of them. At the same time, some board members might not ask the right questions because they don't have enough information to frame the most pertinent questions.

While the rationale for a culture of inquiry is compelling, changes will not occur as a result of simply saying, "Let's have a culture of inquiry." It requires not only a change of mindset but also a committed effort from the group (and a rigorous, disciplined effort from the chief executive, the board chair, and other board officers) to surmount the prevailing norms and the steady turnover of board members. For board members who come with an appreciation for the way in which the board's social system influences its performance, this approach will resonate. Others will dismiss the need to attend to the social fabric of the board as the "soft" stuff.

To paraphrase Mark Twain, most nonprofit leaders advocate progress in governance — it's just change they can't stand. While major governance changes cannot be made quickly unless they are reactions to catastrophe, many nonprofit leaders have raised the governance bar. A growing number of nonprofit organizations have instituted major changes with courage, candor, communication, and the will to act. In other cases, small, well-focused actions have produced significant enduring improvements. A board that embraces continuous learning is more likely to surmount the natural resistance to change because it is receptive to best practices and opportunities to strengthen the way in which the board works together as a group.

While the nature of culture is increasingly recognized in management literature as a distinguishing variable in high performing groups, it is much easier to define the desired results of a culture of inquiry than it is to create the results. The challenge for boards lies not in merely accepting the value of a culture of inquiry but in incorporating its practices into boardroom behavior. A culture of inquiry may appeal to many, but it is a delusional goal without the presence of three things: the tools to practice it, the discipline of leaders such as the chief executive and board chair to make it happen, and the will to act when it needs fine-tuning or a major overhaul.

Four Essential Building Blocks

The following four chapters describe the way in which successful leaders enlist four building blocks to shape a culture of inquiry: trust, information sharing, teamwork, and dialogue. To help the reader think aspirationally and act practically, the format for each block is to introduce why it matters, to illustrate what the board looks like when this building block is present, and to provide concrete strategies to move each building block from theory to practice. This book is not intended to be prescriptive; instead it offers multiple suggestions that are meant to prompt new thinking about board culture. The book is intended to serve as a resource on proven practices of boards that strive to operate at the highest level of their collective capacity.

3.

Trust

Trust begins the process of developing a culture of inquiry. Trust is only partially rooted in character. It requires time to communicate it by example and to forge it by experience. For a board to hold the organization it governs in trust, board members need to trust one another and the chief executive. An atmosphere of trust yields significant rewards. It enables board and staff to support and challenge one another by asking and answering tough questions that serve the organization's interest. It inspires a commitment to the organization's work that encourages board members to stay informed and be engaged. It fosters attention to results, which prompts board members to ask what the organization is accomplishing (or not). And it promotes process transparency, or access to information every board member needs for responsible stewardship.

Creating and sustaining a culture of trust, loyalty, and mutual respect can be a challenge because it must survive the flux of rotating board membership, the infrequency of board meetings, and the distance of most boards from the organization's daily operations. While some boards reelect members to multiple terms, it is not unusual to have term limits requiring one-third of a board to turn over annually. In some organizations, the board chair position changes as much as yearly. Each new board chair brings a different personal style and needs that do not always mesh naturally with those of the chief executive or the rest of the board. When a board meets infrequently and members come from different regions, they are less likely to benefit from the social opportunities that help them become better acquainted with board colleagues and the chief executive.

Boards that are most successful in building and sustaining the trust that supports a culture of inquiry do not do so accidentally or incidentally. Their leaders create opportunities to nurture collective leadership among all board members, and in the process they promote mutual respect and a collaborative spirit. A good board chair will ensure that decisions reflect the wisdom of the entire board, not just the will of a few members. A good chief executive will not play favorites with board members by selectively sharing or withholding information. Legal authority for governance tasks such as the oversight of the chief executive's performance and the setting of executive compensation ultimately resides in the full board, not in a subset of its members. Any board member who wishes detailed information about any aspect of the transactions that relate to the board's collective fiduciary responsibilities should have equal access to the information. These issues and others are addressed in more detail throughout this book.

Tools for Creating an Environment of Trust

1. Set the tone from the top.

As the late, great Peter Drucker used to remind us, good people with good intentions are not enough. Developing a culture of inquiry will be virtually impossible if the chief executive and the board chair do not embrace, model, and actively monitor it. If you try to impose a culture of inquiry on a top-down, hierarchical board, it probably will not take hold.

The relationship between the board chair and the chief executive is a critical component of building trust, especially since these two individuals are the primary board "culture shapers." As they consciously help one another meet their responsibilities, they create opportunities to improve the board's performance and advance the organization. The most constructive board chair–chief executive relationships are built on trust and mutual respect, the ability to balance governance and management, and regular, open, and honest communication. As gatekeepers, the two leaders also determine whether to share information in a timely and open way with all board members or to distribute it only to a select subset of the board.

Tasks for the Chief Executive

Since the board chair changes more often than the chief executive (at least in most organizations), the executive probably will have to make the most adjustments to new styles and communication needs. Each new chair brings different styles and preferences to the position. The savvy chief executive will seek ways to clarify mutual expectations by inviting the new chair to address some of these questions:

- What does a relationship based on mutual trust look like to you?

- What can we do to minimize surprises, anticipate governance challenges before they become problems, and encourage candid communication between the two of us?

- What is your preferred mode of communication between board meetings?

- How will you most need my help during the coming year?

- What other steps can we take to strengthen our relationship as board chair and chief executive?

Trust and mutual respect do not magically appear at the beginning of a chair's or chief executive's term. One executive gets to know each new board chair by traveling to his or her hometown and spending a day observing him or her at work. Another executive takes the chair-elect to at least one governance workshop or symposium that focuses on the interactions of this leadership team. This experience helps them get to know one another a little better at a personal level while learning from peers. At many organizations, the chair or chief executive takes the time to meet individually with board members at least once a year to make sure that each person feels a sense of inclusiveness and access to the leadership team.

Tasks for the Board Chair

The board chair plays a key role in either reinforcing or undermining norms of behavior that stimulate trust. The chair's work takes place in multiple places including

- before the meeting when he or she collaborates with the chief executive to prepare the agenda

- during the meeting when he or she facilitates discussion

- after the meeting when he or she reviews meeting evaluations and follows up with board members who have concerns

- between board meetings as a sounding board for the chief executive or a designated spokesperson for the board

To create a sense of respect, trust, and camaraderie, a good chair must invite discussion, draw out all members to participate, and not cut off conversation prematurely. A board chair will diminish trust and impede a culture of inquiry by ignoring board members who chronically tune out, dominate, or demonstrate disruptive behavior. Effective chairs use a combination of personal and group persuasion to ensure that all voices are heard and meaningfully engaged. A chair can privately encourage a board member to speak up or publicly ask for his or her opinion. A chair can also create more time to hear from each board member by encouraging small-group discussions or going around the table at board meetings to have everyone offer an opinion on a particular question.

Sometimes board chairs seek others who can offset their limitations and complement their strengths. Chairs who are uncomfortable with dissenting views or unwilling to handle disruptive board members may turn to other members or the chief executive for coaching. Or they might invite their more-skilled peers or a trained facilitator to lead critical board-meeting sessions that require an engaged board to question assumptions constructively, seek additional information, and express differing viewpoints.

2. AGREE ON RULES OF ENGAGEMENT.

Board members' behavior can undermine a culture of inquiry. Unwritten rules and patterns — leadership consultant Margaret Wheatley calls them the "underlying agreements we have made about how we will be together" — evolve slowly and often imperceptibly. Attempting to create a higher degree of trust may require trying to change the behavior of certain individuals, especially those who are set in their ways, used to calling the shots, and more skilled at muffling conflict than at voicing differences.

Some chief executives have a tendency to suppress criticism and conflict. The motives for doing so can range from a low tolerance for conflict to a perception of the board as a nuisance to be marginalized. Regardless of the motive, the dangers are multiple. The best solutions may not be put on the table, the potential pitfalls and problems may not be identified in advance, and individual board members may not support the final decision (and subsequently undermine it) if they don't feel that they have been heard.

A constructive way to cultivate an environment of trust is to ask board members what norms of behavior they wish to honor during their work together. A growing number of organizations have developed rules of engagement that they share with new board members and revisit regularly to empower the board. If each board member contributes his or her perceptions to a shared set of agreements about how the board should operate, the group as a whole has a better chance of devising an inclusive, productive, and civil way of "being together." While it is tempting merely to borrow thoughtful rules of engagement developed by another organization, these kinds of agreements won't be successful unless board members create and monitor their own rules.

Some board chairs like to remind board members of their group norms at the start of every board meeting. The board of the International Society for Performance Improvement, an association dedicated to improving productivity and performance in the workplace, makes its rules of engagement highly visible by printing them on

HOW ONE BOARD SETS RULES OF ENGAGEMENT

BOARD BEHAVIORS AND PROCESSES

Discussions

- Feel free to raise an issue/concern, and expect a considerate reply.

- Respect and learn from differences of opinion.

- Build on each other's ideas.

- Value the contributions of all members.

- Ensure that every person has expressed his/her views.

- Don't pontificate.

Decisions

- There are no reprisals for speaking your mind.

- It's okay to agree to disagree.

- Challenge groupthink.

- Check assumptions before running with or arguing against someone else's idea.

- Commit to board decisions.

- Disagree, then commit.

- Seek and respect the opinion or recommendation of staff management.

Interaction with ISPI Members

- It's okay to solicit ideas from the membership. Doing so does not violate board integrity.

- Individual members should not make commitments for the board.

- In the board meeting location, board members may participate in an event that has strategic advantage.

placemats (along with the mission, vision, decision processes, and strategic priorities) that are the first thing board members see when they sit down at the start of a meeting (see How One Board Sets Rules of Engagement).

One indicator of success is whether board members feel comfortable calling attention to breaches or violations of their rules of engagement. Troublesome board members who act out without consequences end up being rewarded for their disruptive behavior. What board members say and do after they leave the boardroom is also important because it demonstrates whether there is respect for the integrity of the decision-making process and sustainable consensus on board actions.

3. HELP BOARD MEMBERS GET TO KNOW EACH OTHER.

It is difficult to build trust in a group that works together only within the confines of official board meetings. Board members who have had opportunities to get to know each other outside the boardroom are better able to work as colleagues in pursuit of the mission. When a board member wants to raise a different opinion, he or she is

---

Interaction with Fellow Board Members

- Hold each other accountable (the executive director is not the board police).

- Provide feedback. If the feedback is specific, it should be given one-on-one. Speak in the first person only, not second-hand.

Before Meetings

- Attend all agreed-upon meetings and come prepared.

- Read documentation prior to meetings.

- Identify the outcome for proposed agenda items.

During Meetings

- Develop shared meaning on old/new ideas.

- Check to see that we're on the same page.

- Seek additional information or data before stating opinion as fact.

- Clarify content, implications, fit to strategic plan, and consequences.

- Test agreements frequently.

- Take time to look at the long-range view.

- Ensure board committees/work groups are given proper authority and resources for completion of assignments.

- Maintain a strategic focus and establish supporting policy.

- Keep discussions inside the boardroom confidential.

After Meetings

- Minutes will capture agreements, actions/timing, and responsibilities.

- Follow up with stakeholders.

Source: International Society for Performance Improvement

more likely to speak up among people who are not just passing acquaintances. Yet board members often come and go from their meetings without ever learning more about those who sit with them at the table.

Having fun together is not a waste of time. Informal interaction with board colleagues builds social capital, promotes teamwork, and creates greater loyalty and desire on the part of board members to contribute as a group. To overcome the potential barriers of distance, diversity, demographics, and varying years of service, there are a number of ways to help board members get to know each other on a personal level and foster trust and mutual respect in their exchanges:

- Invite board members to introduce themselves at board meetings and share something that their colleagues are not likely to know about them. This technique helps board colleagues learn about professional interests and accomplishments, personal passions from hobbies to philanthropic interests, community involvement, or significant family events.

- Go around the room at the start of a meeting to invite board members to do a brief "check-in" about something that has happened in their lives since the last meeting that relates to their board service.

- Have the professional who staffs the board produce an annual notebook that includes an up-to-date biographical sketch on each board member with background about his or her expertise and interests.

- Host a lunch or dinner before or after a board meeting every quarter or twice a year. Invite members of the management team and board members, as well as all their significant others. The organization pays for the cost of the dinner, so everyone can attend regardless of expense limitations.

- Schedule board retreats to allow the board to step back from its typical business routine and focus on a big issue, including reflection on its own performance. While retreats are excellent forums for giving board members more time to get to know each other and build team play, these social occasions and informal interactions also contribute to mutual trust and respect by inviting board members to explore common interests and appreciate other facets of their colleagues' personalities and perspectives.

4. CREATE THE CONDITIONS THAT SUPPORT CANDOR AND CONSENSUS.

It is difficult, if not impossible, to build trust in an atmosphere where board members cannot engage in candid discussions of complex issues and instead suppress their views or channel dissent in destructive ways. To avoid this mindset, some boards appoint a devil's advocate. Others wisely separate discussion and debate from action by inviting the board to discuss the issue at one meeting, allowing time between meetings to process or collect additional information, and taking a vote at the next meeting.

Governance consultant Maureen Robinson tells this story: "I know of a terrific [nonprofit] organization with an energetic and charismatic executive who produced outstanding results year after year. But a moment came when the executive found it harder and harder to pull rabbits out of the hat and even more difficult to admit this to his admiring board. The board, not wanting to appear to doubt the executive's abilities, averted its gaze. Admiration, sympathy, gratitude, and loyalty — all good sentiments in and of themselves — conspired in the boardroom to undo an organization."[4]

To get to consensus, it is helpful to give board members an opportunity to put their points of view on the table and consider the alternatives and consequences of each choice. The chair's skills as a facilitator, the way the meeting is structured, and the kind of information the board is provided to reach a decision (all practices covered in this book) will contribute to the degree to which board members are willing to generate options, share questions, and challenge assumptions. One board deliberately defers votes on important issues until it takes a straw poll. Each board member is asked literally to hold up a straw following the informal discussion to get a sense of the board and determine how much further discussion and debate are needed.

One way to build trust and evaluate the integrity of the process that has produced consensus is to ensure that board members can answer all the following questions affirmatively after the vote:

- I was able to voice my viewpoint.

- I believe that other board members understood my viewpoint.

- I believe that I understood other board members' viewpoints.

- Whether or not I prefer this decision, I support it because the board came to it in an open, fair, and inclusive manner.

Negative answers to any of the above questions can influence the level of civility and trust in the boardroom. Board members who understand that opponents may disagree in good faith are in a better position to work together to find areas of agreement and ways to forge consensus. If a board is having trouble developing the kind of decision-making process that builds sustainable agreements, the chief executive and board chair should ask themselves and the members of the board what they can do to create this climate.

---

4. Maureen Robinson, "Declaration of Independence," *Board Member*, March/April 2007.

4.

Information Sharing

Board members deserve timely, appropriate, and understandable materials before being asked to deliberate or decide. A culture of inquiry does not require board members to continually debate or dissent. It does require regular opportunities for board members to review information that helps them question and inquire rather than simply advocate and decide.

The steady thump of the rubber stamp in the boardroom can be a subliminal sign to new board members that recommendations for action should automatically be treated as signed, sealed, and delivered before the vote is taken. When the board spends too much time reviewing the background of a recommendation for action, this behavior may signal that board members have not received sufficient information to make a knowledgeable decision. It could also mean that they have not done their homework by reading the advance materials, or that they are simply not ready to make a decision. When a board has relevant background information that explains how a recommendation was developed, it is more likely to engage in informed decision making.

Many board members complain that the information they get before board meetings is too much, too little, or too late. The staff often argues that while board members ask for more information, they don't always read the materials provided. What is clear from most collective complaints — and from the growing degree of upper-body strength needed to transport board materials to and from meetings — is that too many boards do not receive information tailored to their governance responsibilities. For example, if the modification of a critical new initiative with governance implications is on the agenda, a verbatim list of all of the comments that have been shared on the initiative may not help the board move forward. Materials that review what the initiative is designed to achieve, summarize the results, and frame questions that assess the impact constitute governance information.

Governing boards do not need more information. Their members do need to be more thoughtful and assertive about the amount and type of information they need to be good stewards and strategic thinkers. Administrative data developed for staff use should not simply be recycled into the board packet. It is difficult for board members to participate in informed deliberations and make decisions if they receive a lot of material that is not organized in a useful way.

Barry S. Bader, a governance consultant specializing in health care institutions, notes the distinguishing characteristics of an effective board information system:

- designed to help the board understand the big picture

- directly related to helping the board discharge its responsibilities

- clear and concise, because board members have limited time to analyze information

- contextual, meaning that current information is compared with projections, trends, or comparison groups, with variances highlighted

- accurate and credible, because the board has ultimate accountability for the organization's existence

Boards that don't consistently look at the big picture and ask the right questions may be constrained not just by insufficient information, but by bounded awareness — the failure to seek, use, and share information. Max Bazerman and Dolly Chugh explain the phenomenon this way in the January 2006 edition of *Harvard Business Review*: "First, executives may fail to see or seek out key information needed to make a sound decision. Second, they may fail to use the information they do see because they aren't aware of its relevance. Finally, executives may fail to share information with others, thereby bounding the organization's awareness." A nonprofit board can easily fall into the same trap. Bazerman and Chugh recommend a four-step process to help individuals increase their awareness of organizational issues, challenges, and risks (see Decisions without Blinders on page 25).

TOOLS FOR SHARING INFORMATION

1. USE BOARD ORIENTATION AS AN INFORMATION-SHARING OPPORTUNITY.

Board orientation is an excellent forum for sharing information early and well with new board members so that they can participate fully from the start. Orientation should offer information about the organization, the field it serves, and the board's role and responsibilities. It should also explain important organizational norms for how the board operates and address subtle issues that will help newcomers understand the work they are asked to do.

A growing number of boards now invite new and veteran board members alike to participate in board orientation. In this case, the focus of the agenda shifts to preparing the incoming board for the work ahead. This has the added benefit of helping the members of the next class of board members get to know the group before the new board members attend their first board meeting.

One educational organization prepares a list of "Questions from Newcomers: Answers from Veteran Board Members" that provides answers to questions such as:

- Who sits where? Is it OK to get up and go to the bathroom or get a cup of coffee? What's the dress code?

- Is it acceptable to question or appear to disagree with staff, the chief executive, the board chair, or other board members?

- Is it permissible to question or to vote against a committee recommendation?

- How formal or informal is the decision making? Do we follow Robert's Rules? Will I be "out of order"?

- Does the board have executive sessions? What are the protocol and agenda for these sessions?

DECISIONS WITHOUT BLINDERS

1. See information.

   - Know what you are looking for, and train your eyes. Secret Service agents can scan a crowd to recognize risks. Business executives can do something similar by asking questions like "What if our strategy is wrong? How would we know?" Simply asking the question will force you to pay attention to areas you're typically unaware of.

   - Develop (or pay for) an outsider's perspective. Ask this person or group to tell you things you don't see from your vantage point. Even if you know you can't implement radical recommendations, having more data at hand is critical.

2. Seek information.

   - Challenge the absence of disconfirming evidence. Receiving recommendations without contradictory data is a red flag indicating that your team members are falling prey to bounded awareness. Assign someone to play the role of devil's inquisitor (a person who asks questions, as opposed to a devil's advocate who argues an alternative point of view).

   - Undersearch in most contexts, but oversearch in important contexts. Think about the implications of an error; if it would be extremely difficult to recover from, then oversearching is a wise strategy.

3. Use information.

   - Unpack the situation. Make sure you're not overemphasizing one focal event and discounting other relevant information. By consciously thinking about the full context of your situation, you're less likely to disregard important data.

   - Assume that the information you need exists in your organization. It often does, and if you approach it with that mindset, you're more likely to discover it.

4. Share information.

   - Everyone has unique information; ask for it explicitly. Meeting agendas for top executives should require updates from all members, thus increasing the probability that important individual information is shared.

   - Create structures that make information sharing the default. Consider making one individual responsible for assembling information from many sources.

At Tulane University, board orientation has clear information-sharing purposes. President Scott Cowen describes the process developed to help trustees get background information on important issues of concern to them: "There are three primary goals to the [orientation] sessions. The first is to review, in detail, the financial status of the university and its administrative units. Second, we review the strategic plan and the performance measures used to track our progress. Finally, we use the sessions to introduce trustees to a few of the high-profile risk areas of the university, such as health-related areas and intellectual property."[5]

At another organization, new board members participate in a *Jeopardy*-style panel in which they are invited to ask questions on topics related to the organization's mission, activities, infrastructure, and governance documents. This approach turned out to be lively, informative, and fun for everyone.

2. LABEL AGENDA ITEMS TO GUIDE BOARD CONSIDERATION.

A board with a culture of inquiry strikes an appropriate balance in giving board members the right things to talk about and helping them talk about those things in a constructive way. Board chairs and chief executives can foster a culture of inquiry by ensuring that board members have appropriate background materials for each agenda item. One way to do this is to help board members distinguish the purpose of these materials and the subsequent response invited from the board. The purpose can be

- communication to keep the board informed

- consultation on an action that may not require the board's formal approval

- decision making on a matter that the board is authorized or invited to vote on

It is becoming more common for boards to explicitly label (and allot a specific time to) each item on the board agenda to help board members understand how it is related to the board's or the organization's strategic priorities and what deliverable the board is being asked to provide. For example, one board categorizes agenda items in four domains: fiduciary, strategic, board development, or board business. Another organization tries to link as many agenda items as possible to the directions, priorities, and metrics from its most recent strategic plan. The value of labeling board agenda items extends beyond helping board members anticipate what they are expected to do with the item. This kind of intention reduces the likelihood of "administrivia" creeping into board meetings and illuminates the kind of information the board needs to address each agenda item.

3. PROVIDE CONTEXTUAL INFORMATION.

To avoid isolated or insular thinking, the board should have access to contextual intelligence on topics and issues they must tackle. In addition to visits with other boards, helpful techniques include attendance at educational programs on governance, mini-seminars, presentations by trustees or professionals from other

---

5. Scott Cowen, "Don't Be Known as Enron U.," *Trusteeship*, July/August 2002.

organizations that faced a similar problem, and consultation with respected outsiders. This kind of information may come from the following sources:

- relevant articles about what's happening in the organization's field, distributed regularly to board members

- a brief chief executive's report in between meetings to keep board members up to date and reduce their own "show and tell" time at board meetings

- guest speakers at meetings to provide continuing education about topics related to the organization's mission, programs, and community

- the results of an environmental scan, a survey on trends in the mission area, or new reports that shine a light on effective practices

The bounded awareness phenomenon described earlier in this chapter can cause board members to ignore critical information when making decisions. Fortunately, information sources abound, especially because organizations related to the nonprofit sector have content-rich Web sites. Umbrella organizations such as ASAE & The Center for Association Leadership have produced useful reports such as *Mapping the Future* and *7 Measures of Success* that provide trends and benchmarks to fuel stimulating discussions as a prelude to a board retreat or a strategic planning process.

The most cohesive *and* the most polarized boards can benefit from consulting outside experts or retaining professionals for advice on consequential issues for which board members do not have sufficient expertise. Multifaceted strategic issues that come before the board often need to be examined from several perspectives rather than viewed through one frame or too many like-minded perspectives. Presentations to the board by external experts or nonprofit leaders from other organizations that faced similar problems can be helpful.

When going to external sources for information, don't forget to mine the rich experiences of your own board members. You may be surprised and delighted by the precious social, political, and intellectual capital that your board members have been withholding — not because they are stingy, but simply because they have not been invited to share it or accorded the respect of having others genuinely listen to it when they do. Instead of basing their decisions exclusively on what the organizational or board leaders impart, board members should be invited to contribute to the information flow.

4. PRESENT INFORMATION IN A FORMAT THAT WORKS FOR THE BOARD.

For the kinds of strategic unresolved board agenda items that benefit most from a culture of inquiry, it is essential to organize background materials in formats that encourage board members to rethink assumptions, frame questions, generate alternative solutions, and engage in constructive and candid deliberation.

For example, the National Court Reporters Association follows this set format to frame issues that its board must deliberate or take action on:

Issue: A single sentence or title that identifies the topic to be addressed.

Background: A brief paragraph or two that describe how the issue emerged, summarize any past history that would be useful in creating a context for considering the issue, and provide current status.

Discussion: An outline and brief discussion of the various options available, ramifications of action (or inaction), pros and cons, and other general analysis.

Objective(s): An explicit statement of the action being requested from the board.

For example:

- formal board action, for which a draft motion is presented

- more general direction from the board on desired next steps for the committee/staff

- an item to be addressed as a strategic dialogue

Attachments: Any relevant backup material (correspondence, data, reports, etc.) that might assist the board in making an informed decision should be listed attached to the issue paper.

Board members should also have a written summary of the ideas generated by the board outside of a formal business session, even though it may not have concluded with board consensus. For example, the summary of a discussion on a strategic issue might frame the issue, identify key discussion points and options considered at a previous meeting, and conclude with recommendations on next steps. While this summary should not be construed as an action plan, it helps the board build on the discussion and move forward the next time it comes up on the agenda, rather than start over again.

The Meyer Foundation makes sure its board has meaningful discussions about substantive policy issues at every meeting by preparing "greens" — in-depth topic papers that conclude with questions for the board. Printed on green paper to make sure they stand out to board members perusing the board book, these documents are prepared by staff members with expertise about each topic. Based on evidence collected from discussions with fellow program officers and senior staff, meetings with grantees, and grantees' final reports, program officers summarize the foundation's grantmaking history in a particular area and make recommendations for possible changes. Occasionally they write about areas fairly new to the foundation to ask for the board's input on whether dollars should be shifted to different fields.

Staff members are present if board members have questions, but the discussion is primarily conducted by board members who bring their own professional and civic experiences to the table. Often the board offers provisional opinions about a topic but asks staff to investigate further and report back at a future board meeting. Greens give the board the opportunity to gain a deeper understanding of the range of issues that Meyer grantees address, and board discussion gives staff members policy recommendations they can use to shape their work.

5.

Teamwork

In *The Wisdom of Teams: Creating the High-Performance Organization*, Jon R. Katzenbach and Douglas K. Smith argue that whenever there is a need for a real-time combination of multiple skills, experiences, and judgments, teams outperform a collection of individuals with defined roles and responsibilities. At the top of their team performance curve, they describe a high-performance team as "a group of people with complementary skills who are equally committed to a common purpose, performance goals, and approach for which they hold themselves mutually accountable."[6]

The high-performance board, like the high-performance team, does not simply evolve. An assembly of talented, competent individuals does not automatically result in a talented, competent board. In their seminal work on nonprofit boards, the research team of Richard P. Chait, William P. Holland, and Barbara E. Taylor found that without an intentional effort to develop the capacity of the individuals on a board to work as a group, their natural inclinations actually pull them toward the very things we wring our hands about — away from long-term challenges toward immediate concerns, away from strategy toward operations, and away from collective actions toward individual actions.[7] Board members have this tendency not only because team building takes time but also because they are likely to be doers who are used to being rewarded for the operational as well as the strategic tasks they perform in their day jobs, direct service volunteer work, or other roles. The typical board can be, in Chait's apt metaphor, a "huddle of quarterbacks."

To add to the forces against teamwork, board members do not necessarily receive formal preparation for their role, nor do they know each other well or have much in common besides their positions on the board. If they are not given opportunities to build relationships, they can become an artificial or shallow team that doesn't enjoy the benefit of regular interaction. Some leaders dismiss the stuff of relationships and social dynamics as simply a function of the natural gifts or deficiencies that individuals bring to their board service. The best board chairs and chief executives, however, actively monitor how the board operates as a social system. (See chapter 2 for more on the importance of relationship building among board members.)

A board may stay in what Bruce Tuckman describes as the forming stage of group dynamics, rather than moving on to what he calls the storming, norming, and performing stages (see How Groups Develop). A board that never moves beyond forming may not be capable of engaging in a culture of inquiry. Any discussion, situation, or controversy may result in apathy (if members do not feel like their peers

---

6. Jon R. Katzenbach and Douglas K. Smith, *The Wisdom of Teams: Creating the High-Performance Organization* (New York: HarperBusiness, 1994).

7. Richard P. Chait, William P. Ryan, and Barbara E. Taylor, *Improving the Performance of Nonprofit Boards* (Phoenix: American Council on Education Oryx Press Series on Higher Education, 1996).

know them or care about their opinions) or extreme positions that create polarization (if the board as a whole has not coalesced into a high-performing group with common goals and collective accountability).

The most illuminating examples of what can happen when board members — whether nonprofit or for-profit — do not engage in effective team play can be found in the colossal governance breakdowns at companies such as Enron, WorldCom, and Tyco (see the Enron example in chapter 1). When corporate governance expert Jeffrey Sonnenfeld examined these meltdowns,[8] he found two interesting things. First, the boards of these failed companies actually demonstrated some of the widely accepted governance benchmarks regarding meeting attendance, board size, committee structure, and the management acumen and financial literacy of individual board members. Furthermore, written codes of ethics were in place.

Second, the salient difference between these failed boards and those considered the best in the field relates to group behavior. Sonnenfeld found that what makes a great corporate board great has less to do with adherence to the requirements of the Sarbanes-Oxley Act and more to do with how board members actually function together as a high-performing group. The exceptional boards Sonnenfeld studied demonstrated critical group traits such as a climate of trust and candor among board members and between board and management, a willingness to share information with board members openly and on time, a culture in which board members feel free to challenge one another's assumptions and conclusions, a management team that encourages lively discussions of strategic issues by the board, and a commitment to assessing the performance of the board as a collective group as well as of the individual members.

When high-performing boards emerge in the nonprofit or for-profit sector, they do not spring from the head of Zeus. Their cultures are intentionally and meticulously shaped. The leaders of the most effective boards, according to Chait, Holland, and Taylor, take deliberate steps to transform an assembly of talented individuals into a high-performing team. As a result, these boards demonstrate interpersonal and analytical competencies. They reflect the belief that an inclusive and cohesive board makes better decisions than do individuals. They continuously draw upon members' multiple perspectives to avoid the trap of "groupthink." They foster inclusive relationships from the time a new board member is recruited. And they build in regular opportunities for board development, gathering feedback on their performance and learning from their mistakes.

TOOLS FOR CULTIVATING TEAMWORK

1. DEVELOP A BALANCED BOARD.

Board composition is critical to stewardship, strategic thinking, and the capacity to build a culture of inquiry. Regardless of the method of board selection, the board should weigh in on the knowledge, skills, and perspectives needed in future members

---

8. J. A. Sonnenfeld, "What Makes Great Boards Great?," *Harvard Business Review*, September 2002.

HOW GROUPS DEVELOP

In 1965 Bruce Tuckman introduced his four stages of group development and operation. The process is usually subconscious and not deliberate, but understanding the processes can often facilitate the group's effectiveness. In the governance world, boards are continually changing as new members and leaders move back and forth into stages such as forming and storming. The board chair and the chief executive should recognize that the "performing" stage is not a natural act and be ready to help the board progress.

Stage 1: Forming — Individual behavior is influenced by each person's desire to be accepted and avoid conflict. The group avoids serious issues or bad feelings, and individuals concentrate on business such as dividing tasks and determining logistics. Meanwhile, individuals in the group are learning about each other and forming impressions of the group.

Stage 2: Storming — When the group starts working on real issues, some initial politeness and patience dissolve. Some members of the group are enthusiastic about delving into meaningful work, while others prefer the comfort of Stage 1 and will gloss over confrontation. Conflict may remain buried.

Stage 3: Norming — Once the standards for behavior in the group have been established and the group understands its responsibilities, members know each other better and value their peers' abilities and contributions. Individuals respect each other, listen to others' views, and support their colleagues. Members may feel a stronger sense of commitment to a cohesive group.

Stage 4: Performing — Although not all groups reach this stage, performing is characterized by flexibility, trust, and interdependence. Members know each other well and work together effectively. Morale is high, and members are loyal to the group and identify strongly with it. Members can direct their energy to accomplishing their goals instead of building the team.

A decade after introducing these principles, Tuckman added another stage.

Stage 5: Adjourning — At some point many groups need to disband, and this stage represents accomplishment of a group's goal and a positive conclusion of the work of the group.

Sources: Bruce W. Tuckman, "Developmental Sequence in Small Groups," *Psychological Bulletin* 63 (1965): 384-99; Tuckman and Mary Ann C. Jensen, "Stages of Small-Group Development Revisited," *Group and Organization Studies* 2, no. 4 (December 1977): 419-26.

to renew and strengthen the board to add the greatest value. Once a year, the governance committee should seek the board's guidance to assess future organizational needs, current board competencies, and diversity criteria for the next class of board members. In addition to looking for professional skills and demographic criteria that will ensure diversity in board composition, some governance committees look more closely at personal traits that will advance the work of the board, such as experience with governance, the ability to think strategically, and the commitment to work effectively within the group process of a collective decision-making body.

Every bit as important are interpersonal, analytical, and emotional competencies, which are more difficult to describe on paper. These qualities can only be detected by direct observation or candid feedback from someone who has worked with a particular individual within a group. For example, a board may seek to balance individuals who are talkative or argumentative with those who are pensive and reflective. Boards also benefit from members who employ pragmatism, logic, and objectivity as well as intuition, flexibility, and empathy. Subtle underlying behavioral traits matter, too, such as how a person communicates his or her opposing point of view (see Diversity That Builds a Culture of Inquiry).

These qualities are not mutually exclusive, but the point is that not all board members bring the kind of interpersonal and group process skills to the board table that have been associated with emotional intelligence. For example, some board members may have a greater aptitude for working in an entrepreneurial or hierarchical environment that does not value inclusiveness and collective decision making. Others who are brilliantly analytical and supremely rational may have a more difficult time building rapport with peers or finding common ground to move from process to action.

2. CULTIVATE DISCUSSION SKILLS.

Once a board of talented, trustworthy, team-willing players has been assembled, it's essential to ensure that they work effectively as a group and that their time together is spent productively. Carol Weisman, a board consultant, once lamented, in her wry manner, that she observed stronger team building mechanisms in urban youth gangs during her early career as a social worker. Compared to nonprofit boards, gangs typically set clearer expectations for new members, developed more intentional methods for orientation and continuing education, and defined clearer metrics for monitoring the performance of the group and its individual members!

As noted in chapter 2, the chief executive's and chair's roles are critical variables for a culture of inquiry. Together, the chief executive and chair can carry out their roles as the "chief board development officers" by monitoring as well as supporting the culture. Is everyone's voice being heard? Are people listening? Is the atmosphere one where people feel "safe" and comfortable sharing unpopular ideas and questions? Is there an agenda, and does it provide time to focus on what's important? It takes a secure (and courageous) chief executive and chair to keep an eye on all of these elements while being on the lookout for personal agendas or evidence of groupthink or "surface only" harmony. Since the success of the board will be influenced by the chair's ability to facilitate group interaction, it is important to look for this skill set in officer succession planning.

Diversity That Builds a Culture of Inquiry

The following composite personality types illuminate ways that individual board members can contribute to a culture of inquiry. Most people have a combination of traits that may emerge according to the situation. But a board that is completely missing any of these traits — or is too heavily weighted with one or two — will have a harder time governing in a culture of inquiry mode.

The Analyst: Adept at generating conceptual possibilities, sorting through large amounts of information, considering the consequences of proposed actions, and/or analyzing options strategically, objectively, and dispassionately.

The Healthy Skeptic: Enjoys questioning the pros and cons, testing new ideas, playing the devil's advocate, and airing "dissensus" for a good argument that will help surface intelligent doubt and illuminate the issues and the stakes.

The Facilitator: Highly attuned to the needs and emotions of others by encouraging full participation, ensuring that different views are heard, and supporting everyone to do their best thinking. Helps keep the board on track in serving the interests of the organization and the board. (Ideally, facilitator traits are present in the board chair, committee chairs, and individuals designated to lead board discussions.)

The Observer: Good at pointing out to the group insights and observations about board dynamics or other issues that illuminate board performance and get disagreements as well as accomplishments out in the open.

The Caller: Courageous, sensitive, and skillful in calling individuals on questionable or inappropriate actions or disrespectful behaviors, the board's desired norms of behavior, or the welfare of the organization.

The Coach: A cheerleader who celebrates what's working well, motivates the board to do even better, and reminds the group of the common vision, core values, and the interests of the organization.

The Reframer: Skilled in recasting a complex or divisive issue in a new light, ferreting out and framing the real challenge at hand, and opening up new possibilities to shift attention to fertile new ground for realistic options.

The Synthesizer: Quickly distills patterns, core issues, common themes, and long-range perspectives on complex, contentious, or controversial issues that summarize the discussion to help the board advance to the next step and avoid rehashing old ground.

When these qualities are not present in the chair (and when a board agenda item cries out for open discussion and dialogue), consider asking another more skilled board member to facilitate the board discussion. A skilled facilitator can draw out everyone's input in a safe and respectful manner, especially if the chair lacks the group-process skills or objectivity to create this climate.

The following mechanisms can encourage open discussion:

- Take turns. To relieve the committee chair, board chair, or other individual leading the discussion, designate another board member to keep a running list of board members who wish to speak. In that way, no one has to focus on getting the attention of the discussion leader but instead can focus on listening to the discussion. Everyone should get time to speak, and those who have not had a chance to speak will be more likely to get their turns.

- Use breakout groups. When the board is tackling a particularly tough issue, it can be useful to break into small groups for parts of the discussion. Less-vocal board members may be more willing to speak in small groups and share opinions they fear will be discordant to or challenged by the majority. Each group can select a facilitator to keep the group on track and a reporter to summarize its thinking for the full board.

3. CONDUCT A REGULAR BOARD SELF-ASSESSMENT.

Research in behavioral science, organizational development, and governance provides strong evidence that it is difficult for individuals and institutions to learn without feedback, which has an important effect on performance. When board members decide together that they're going to evaluate their own effectiveness, they're making a commitment to improvement and excellence. While Richard Chait, Jeffrey Sonnenfeld, and other governance gurus highlight the presence of active mechanisms for the board to review its performance as one of the benchmarks of an effective governing board, not all boards embrace reflection until problems surface. Boards that are self-satisfied, complacent, or disinterested in best practices can experience institutional hardening of the arteries. This condition is changing gradually, however, because boards are under growing pressure to model the behavior they expect of others in the organization and because an increasing variety of board evaluation tools is available on the market.

Well-planned and well-led board self-assessments help a board explore the secrets of how a group of high-achieving individuals from various walks of life can come together to function as a board. A board can use a number of formal and informal mechanisms to enlist feedback on its performance:

- dialogue on a dimension of the board's work at a special forum, retreat, or regular board meeting

- reflective discussion of critical incidents to learn from mistakes or accomplishments

- exit interviews with board members who have completed their terms

- feedback solicited in a questionnaire administered at the conclusion of each board meeting

- board "monitors" who make observations at the end of each meeting about group process, the amount of time the board spends on each issue in the meeting and its relevance to the board's priorities, and other matters of process and content. Board members take turns monitoring meetings.

- internal reviews by an ad hoc or standing committee of the board, such as the governance committee

- board self-assessments — either mini-assessments or more comprehensive ones — that invite board members to assess the board against its discrete responsibilities, structure, and group process

Board members, like most people, are not inclined toward unbiased self-analysis. The value of a formal self-assessment process is that it allots a specific time, a priority, and a forum to self-improvement. A constructive self-assessment yields perceptions about the board's value, strengths, and weaknesses to illuminate how the board views itself.

A cardinal rule for evaluations is to tie them to results. Busy board members want feedback on the assessment findings and specific guidelines for improvement. If an evaluation report winds up on a shelf, the board can easily get assessment fatigue. Board self-assessment should be scheduled at a time when the board and the chief executive are most willing to learn from and act on concrete, assignable, and actionable steps the board can take. Self-assessment can be enhanced by

- clarifying the objectives of the assessment

- customizing a diagnostic tool that is relevant to the board's work for each board member to complete

- scheduling a meeting or retreat dedicated to exploring the results and deciding on ways to improve the board's performance

- preparing a plan of action to follow through on the results

As a corollary to board self-assessment, it is important to have regular opportunities to share accomplishments as well as concerns before problems fester. Options include ongoing board communications, annual chief executive performance assessments, and executive sessions when warranted to foster frank and timely communications.

Board Meeting Evaluations

In addition to conducting full-scale board self-assessments, consider soliciting evaluations from board members after each meeting. These easy, 60-second written evaluations can include up to five questions that probe board members' opinions about the board's work as a whole and about whether their own views and ideas were heard and valued:

- How effective was this board meeting?

- What was the most important decision we made today?

- How much of our time was spent on operational versus strategic matters?

- What was the most interesting or engaging part of today's meeting?

- Was the agenda properly constructed?

- How could this board meeting have been improved?

In some organizations, the board chair leaves time at the end of every meeting for an oral debrief. Regardless of the mode of board self-assessment, the important thing is for the board chair to communicate the results, follow up with any board member who expresses particular concern about an issue or expresses reluctance to speak, and convert the results of this continuous learning tool to actions that need to be taken for continuous improvement.

4. STRENGTHEN THE COMMITTEE STRUCTURE.

Like large teams that must delegate some of their work to subunits, most boards find it difficult to carry out their work without committees. But when committees become silos or mini-boards, they can undermine the collective capacity of the board to function as a high-performing group. When active committees begin to take on lives of their own by generating their own charges, agendas, and work plans that are unrelated to the board's strategic plan or strategic agenda, they can become the tail wagging the dog.

Committee work should be driven by what the board, as a group working together, determines can be accomplished best in committees. Good practice calls for the board chair and chief executive to revisit committee objectives and deliverables once a year to ensure that they derive from the board's strategic agenda, select chairs and committee members who have the best qualifications, and review the viability of the committee structure. This annual assessment may reveal standing committees that have been treated like sacred cows but are no longer functional.

Many boards are reducing the number of standing committees and creating more task forces, advisory groups, and ad hoc committees designed to accomplish specific objectives within specific time frames. Using task forces allows a board greater flexibility in tackling immediate issues. This practice also helps a board focus on institutional and board priorities rather than being bound by tradition. A task force can provide a welcome alternative for busy board members who are able to handle a short-term assignment with a discrete, finite task but not a long-term role on a standing committee. It provides additional opportunities to select members who can advance a culture of inquiry and to screen the competencies of nonboard members of the task force as potential board candidates.

To prevent a committee structure from becoming cumbersome, a zero-based committee structure exercise ensures that form follows function. Every few years, have the board begin hypothetically with no committees. Only after revisiting or determining organizational strategy and priorities can the board establish specific committees and task forces that are aligned with current goals, objectives, and priorities. The underlying assumption for each committee or ad hoc group is that it will disband either when it has met its objective or when the board decides it should disband. The zero-based committee exercise relies on the input of the entire board to ensure that committees actually enhance the board's collective work and to prevent the board from getting trapped in an obsolete model.

THE BOARD-WITHIN-THE-BOARD SYNDROME

A common weakness of large boards or boards that don't meet frequently is to rely on a small group within the board, such as an executive committee, to act as the board within the board (BWB). Well-structured executive committees can be helpful if they understand and execute their circumscribed role — but not when they usurp the role of the board. The following warning signals and interventions help prevent this syndrome.

Red Flag: The BWB makes most of the board's decisions.

Consequences: Board members who do not serve on the BWB feel disenfranchised and can be unpleasantly surprised when they learn of an outcome of a decision for which the collective board is responsible and liable — but not enlisted.

Interventions: Consider whether there is a continuing need for the committee or group that forms the BWB. Explore whether the underlying cause for the BWB relates to the large size of the board, an inadequate committee structure, or other reasons that have created a powerful inner group calling most of the shots.

Red Flag: The BWB meets more frequently than and/or immediately prior to every board meeting.

Consequences: Board members are accountable (and liable) for questionable decisions made by the BWB on their behalf.

Interventions: Confine the work of the BWB to matters that cannot be handled by the full board.

Red Flag: Most board members learn about major governance or management problems when the story hits the front page.

Consequences: Board members not in the "inner loop" continuously question the integrity of the board's decision-making process.

Interventions: Ensure that the meeting agendas, minutes, and decisions of the committee or ad hoc group are sent to the entire board as soon as possible before and after it meets. Invite the entire board to genuinely shape strategy or assess options on decisions offered by committee or ad hoc group.

6.

Dialogue

Louise Diamond of the Institute for Multi-Track Diplomacy describes dialogue in this way: "Dialogue means we sit and talk with each other, especially those with whom we may think we have the greatest differences. However, talking together all too often means debating, discussing with a view to convincing the other, arguing for our point of view, examining pros and cons. In dialogue, the intention is not to advocate but to inquire; not to argue but to explore; not to convince but to discover."

Diamond's practice of dialogue can help restore a more civil tone to the bitter partisanship that surrounds so much discourse in the public arena today. Just think about recent exchanges you have had (or avoided having) with loved ones or professional colleagues with contrary political views on issues you all feel strongly about. How many of them have been characterized by "equality and the absence of coercive influence, listening with empathy, and bringing assumptions into the open" — the three features that Daniel Yankelovich describes to distinguish dialogue from discussion?[9]

Partisanship has also seeped into the boardroom. "Tired ears," a Middle Eastern phrase used to describe people who have stopped listening, can be found on the heads of board members and chief executives who chronically and selectively filter information in a manner that jeopardizes decision making. Chronic patterns of communication within some boards include the lack of interest in hearing opposing views and the tendency to "pronounce" positions rather than engage intellectually on controversial issues. Instead of listening to what is being said to them, too many board members are already thinking about what they plan to say in response.

Dialogue is different from discussion or deliberation. In *The Fifth Discipline*, Peter Senge suggests that the purpose of dialogue is not to decide but to strive to understand in order to create or choose the best possible strategy. In dialogue, the participants are listening first and foremost, working to understand others' points of view instead of waiting to pounce with their own persuasive arguments when others are finished speaking. Participants in dialogue can still stand behind their convictions, but they should explain, and others should listen, reflect, and be willing to share their own assumptions before speculating on those of others.

On contentious issues, it is especially helpful to bring underlying assumptions into the open to clarify whether rituals and value systems that have persisted over the years are still relevant to current realities. Then the rest of the group can ask questions and share other ideas, with the understanding that the group will pay them the same respect. Boards that encourage their members to understand rather than to dismiss each other's arguments are admirable. But they also must have the capacity to

---

9. Daniel Yankelovich, "The Magic of Dialogue," *The Nonprofit Quarterly*, Fall 2001.

choose wisely from among competing imperatives when it comes time to move from dialogue and debate to deciding the best course of action.

Even the best-intentioned board can be led astray by particular personalities who dominate discussions. James Surowiecki's research for *The Wisdom of Crowds* suggests that people who talk a lot in groups become more influential whether or not they have more expertise than others. "Talkativeness may seem like a curious thing to worry about, but in fact talkativeness has a major impact on the kinds of decisions small groups reach. If you talk a lot in a group, people will tend to think of you as influential almost by default."

It turns out that people who talk a lot are also talked to more than others, so they make themselves even more central to the discussion regardless of what their actual contribution might be. One way to tackle the problem of loquacious board members is for the board chair to monitor and adjust the flow of conversation, ensuring that all members have a chance to speak throughout the meeting, even if it means calling on each individual or going around the table to make sure all voices are heard.

TRUE LISTENING

"Dialogue represents a way of working that while perhaps embedded in the genes of our ancestors is new to us. Most people lack real experience of it. We are unused to speaking together openly and consciously, particularly in high-stakes settings, without any intention of somehow possessing for ourselves something of the outcome of these exchanges. We do not know how to participate in such a way that we have not planned in advance what we are going to say, or where we are deliberately inquiring into. We come prepared, well stocked with thoughts, perhaps having sought to prepare others as well. And when the going gets tough, we fall back on argument and debate."

Source: William Isaacs, *Dialogue and the Art of Thinking Together* (New York: Random House, 1999).

In scores of board meetings in which I have participated as a chief executive, board member, or governance consultant, I have watched board members and executives tell their positions and react to their colleagues' views. Less evident are the communication skills of listening to hear the differences and probing for information among colleagues with other opinions. It is not surprising that authentic dialogue is missing in action from many boardrooms, because most of us lack the interest in learning how to do it or the time to practice it. The following tools offer ways to move dialogue from compelling construct to boardroom reality.

"I know that you believe you understand what you think I said, but I'm not sure you realize that what you heard is not what I meant." — Robert McCloskey

TOOLS FOR STIMULATING DIALOGUE

1. REFOCUS BOARD MEETING AGENDAS.

A board's meeting agenda reflects how it values itself. Unfortunately, too many board meetings are highly scripted events in which reports or recommendations are presented with limited opportunities for board members to influence strategy and inadequate information to make informed decisions. Too many boards meet in the same configuration of chairs and in the same pattern of agenda items for every single meeting.

To apply the useful architectural adage that form should follow function, the board chair and chief executive should consider the following questions before planning every meeting agenda:

- What are the key objectives of this meeting?

- What do we want to accomplish at the end of the meeting?

- How will we know if we have been successful?

- What issues are likely to arise that could prevent us from achieving the objectives of the meeting?

- How should the format be organized to achieve the desired objectives and the performance metrics of success?

The answers to these questions might result in a welcome departure from the traditional, report-laden, mind-numbing meetings in which the only skill required of board members is to yawn with their mouths closed. An emerging issue that is high in importance but does not require immediate board action may require a different format such as small breakout groups or a full board discussion to generate ideas and scenarios about the given topic. At other times, a high-stakes or controversial subject may demand special handling. Hiring or firing a chief executive, revisiting mission in a way that might result in cutting major programs, or expanding the organization may warrant conducting discussions in an executive session, as a major agenda item within a board meeting, in a dialogue with an outside facilitator, or at a board retreat.

Here are two ways to mix up mundane board agendas and bring the board into a more substantive conversation:

- Schedule a topic- or issue-based discussion. These discussions (with or without a facilitator) could focus on big issues, allowing the board to focus on the long view. This format is useful for issues that do not require a vote but do require input from all members of the board. In one organization, after the chief executive announced her plans to retire within three years, the board brought in a leadership transition expert to moderate a discussion on the challenges that the next chief executive would face. Other organizations have engaged qualified facilitators rather than content experts to help the board (and staff) consider governance changes, revisit institutional priorities, or consider the implications of new trends.

- Consider thematic meetings. From time to time, it may be helpful to focus an entire meeting on a single, overarching topic that demands the board's time and attention. It could be an urgent matter such as the consideration of a merger, a discussion about where the board wants the organization to go before launching a chief executive search, or a way to begin a strategic planning process. Ambiguous threats — such as the impact of new competition and the growing demand for online versus face-to-face meetings — are good candidates for these kinds of sessions.

In the early years of BoardSource, my board steadily advised me to invest sufficient resources in research and development. To help us think about this concept in a more interesting and informative way, I once invited a leader in the R & D division of a multinational company widely recognized for its innovative and entrepreneurial culture to talk to the board and staff about how the company makes decisions to invest in new products and services. While the contrast in scope between the company and BoardSource was huge, the discussion launched a stimulating dialogue about our institutional risk tolerance and forced us to revisit our core values and financial assumptions.

2. FRAME QUESTIONS RATHER THAN ARGUE THE CASE.

Board members who are asked to sit through boring meetings with predetermined outcomes can't be faulted for yearning to explore emerging issues, stakes, and options related to strategic issues before taking action. But it is irresponsible to expect board members to engage in dialogue unless the materials in the board packet provide a context and focus for the board discussion. It is helpful for the board to have a brief background paper prior to the discussion that could include a summary of the issue, options to consider, and the questions that the board members are being invited to address, such as:

- What do we know from the changing environment (either internal or external) in which the organization works that impinges on this issue?

- What don't we know that will have an impact on this issue?

- How will the needs and expectations of our constituencies (e.g., beneficiaries, members, donors, regulators, staff, and volunteers) most likely be affected by this issue?

- What assets and liabilities within our organizational capacity will affect our ability to address this issue?

- Are there legal, ethical, and moral implications we need to consider for any decision we might have to make?

It is difficult for a group to generate new, often superior, solutions to its problems until it considers views that may be different from its own. It is the very act of asking questions and engaging in conversation with those who think differently that produces new ideas. If you've ever had your thinking challenged and been forced

---

CATALYTIC QUESTIONS

Thoughtful questions for dialogue that invite the board to think more contextually and expansively about a given issue can be incorporated into regular board meetings. Consider posing the kinds of catalytic questions offered by Richard P. Chait, William P. Ryan, and Barbara E. Taylor that invite creativity, exploration, and do not depend largely on data and logic to answer:

- What three adjectives or short phrases best characterize this organization?

- In five years, what will be most strikingly different about this organization?

- On what list, which you would create, would you like this organization to rank at the top?

- Five years from today, what will this organization's key constituents consider the most important legacy of the current board?

- What will be most different about the board or how we govern in five years?

- How would we respond if a donor offered a $50 million endowment to the one organization in our field that had the best idea for becoming a more valuable public asset?

- How would we look as a takeover target by a potential or actual competitor?

- If we could successfully take over another organization, which one would we choose and why?

- What has a competitor done successfully that we would not choose to do as a matter of principle?

- What have we done that a competitor might not do as a matter of principle?

- What headline would we most/least like to see about this organization?

- What is the biggest gap between what the organization claims it is and what it actually is?

Source: Richard P. Chait, William P. Ryan, and Barbara E. Taylor, *Governance as Leadership: Reframing the Work of Nonprofit Boards* (Hoboken, NJ: John Wiley & Sons, 2005).

to defend or abandon your ideas, you know that this questioning, this sort of curiosity, can be uncomfortable. But a common ingredient of a high-functioning board is the presence of individual members who regularly turn to inquiry over advocacy on high stakes or complex issues that cannot be resolved in a perfunctory manner.

Dialogue does not mean that endless options should be projected and debated. Once the right questions have been framed, the board is in a better position to make an informed decision by considering the pros and cons of potential choices before recommending action. If consensus does not emerge, the board can then clarify what kind of additional information is needed before making a decision.

3. LAUNCH A ROBUST DISCUSSION.

Closely aligned with the practice of dialogue is the art of inviting the board to create or generate the definition, questions, and options that relate to a given issue or problem. In *Governance as Leadership*, Chait, Ryan, and Taylor highlight the value of generative thinking as a means of producing solutions based on deliberation and analysis — not on gut feelings or personal preferences. While it may not be practical or productive to enlist this practice at every board meeting, generative thinking is especially suited to embryonic, high-stakes topics or important issues that have not yet been clearly framed. Generative discussions are less appropriate when the board is moving swiftly to a decision or action.

Robust discussion can be noisy, scary, and fast. People talk. They challenge. They build on the ideas of others. They frame and reframe situations to think about them in new ways. Ultimately, it may be about the solution, but the process for getting there helps make the solution stronger. It may even mean making sure they've identified the right problem — possibly something quite different than what they first thought it was. To stimulate the sharing of different points of view, Chait and his colleagues urge the group to start slowly, perhaps by designating someone to play the role of devil's advocate (and then having other board members take turns in this role). This tool is useful for pushing people to examine traditional thinking and question assumptions.

The discussions that result can help everyone begin to frame issues in new ways. While some may experience these techniques as more like games at first, they can be useful in acclimating board members to a different way of thinking and working. Over time the board should become more comfortable conducting discussions in new and more open ways. Chait, Ryan, and Taylor offer the following kinds of techniques for promoting robust discussion.

Mechanisms for Robust Discussion

- **Silent Starts** — Prior to the start of a major discussion, but with advance notice, set aside two minutes for each trustee to anonymously write on an index card the most important question the board and management should consider relevant to the issue at hand. Collect and randomly redistribute the cards. Ask a trustee to read his or her card aloud, and then invite everyone with a card that has a similar question to do the same. Tally the numbers. Continue until all cards have been read aloud. Identify the question(s) most important to the most trustees and any question that, once raised, even if only by one person, the board now recognizes as crucial.

- **One-Minute Memos** — At the conclusion of a major discussion, reserve two to three minutes for trustees to write down, anonymously or not, what they would have said next had there been time to continue the discussion. Collect the cards for review by the board chair and chief executive. No trustee suffers the pain of an undelivered remark or an unstated concern, and the organization's leadership no longer wonders what remained on the trustees' minds.

- **Future Perfect History** — In breakout groups, develop a narrative that explains in the future perfect tense how the organization moved from its current state to an envisioned state. For example, five years from now the college will have achieved greater student and faculty diversity as a result of taking the following steps. Compare the story lines for common pathways as well as attractive, imaginative "detours."

- **Counterpoints** — Randomly designate two to three trustees to make the most powerful counterarguments to initial recommendations or embryonic consensus. Or ask management to present the strongest case against (as well as for) a staff recommendation.

- **Role Plays** — Ask subsets of the board to assume the perspective of different constituent groups likely to be affected by the issue at hand. How would these stakeholders frame the issue and define a successful outcome? What would each group regard as a worst-case scenario? The role play would be enhanced if all trustees were asked in advance to meet informally with one or two such constituents.

- **Breakouts** — Small groups expand available "airtime," ease participation by reticent trustees, and counter "groupthink." On topics of substantive, strategic, or symbolic significance, small groups, even within 30 minutes, can raise important considerations. Do we have the right questions? How else might the issue be framed? What values are at stake? What would constitute a successful outcome? In plenary session, the board can search for consensus, conflicts, and a better understanding of the matter at hand.

- **Simulations** — Trustees can simulate some decisions, not to second-guess the decision but to provoke discussion about the trade-offs that management faces. For example, trustees of an independent college or school could review the redacted applications of the next 20 students who would have been admitted last year if the institution opted for larger enrollments and additional revenues rather than greater selectivity and higher quality.

- **Surveys** — The board can administer an anonymous survey prior to discussion of a major issue. For instance,

  - What should be atop the board's agenda next year?

  - What are the most attractive, least attractive, most worrisome aspects of the proposed strategic plan?

- What external factors will most affect the organization in the next year?

- What are we overlooking at the organization's peril?

- What is the most valuable step we could take to be a better board?

The answers would be collated for board discussion. The discussion would not start in response to the first person to speak on an issue, but by an analysis of the collective responses.[10]

WHAT CONSTITUTES AGREEMENT?

Dr. Mardy Grothe, a psychologist and writer of word and language books observes, "It is often said that understanding does not indicate agreement. It is less well accepted, but also true that agreement does not always indicate understanding."

---

4. HELP BOARD MEMBERS PRACTICE CONSTRUCTIVE DISSENT.

Another principle of exceptional boards is independent-mindedness — the ability of board members to put the interests of the organization above all else when making decisions. While board members should respect formal and legal lines of authority, they must also be free to make their own judgments. In doing so, they may have to advance a point of view different from that of the chief executive and other staff and board members, and they may have to set aside their personal agendas. Yet one often finds "dysfunctional politeness" in the boardroom, a phenomenon that can create a Petri dish in which problems fester.

Board members are individually accountable to one another for civility. As noted in chapter 4, it is helpful to include individuals on the board who will respectfully express healthy skepticism or intelligent doubt during important deliberations. These board members can model for their colleagues how to disagree by focusing on the issue rather by interpreting the difference of opinion as a character flaw in the other person. Engaging in what Patrick Lencioni calls "productive ideological conflict" — rather than destructive fighting, relationship conflict, or interpersonal politics — is essential to dialogue.

Constructive dissent invites individuals with different points of view to attack the issue rather than each other and to maintain civility. It also increases the probability that the group will reach sustainable agreements, whether or not the final decision is unanimous. Destructive dissent, on the other hand, occurs either when board members attack individuals (rather than the issues) with different points of view or when they take their opposing views outside of the boardroom. When members

---

10. Richard P. Chait, William P. Ryan, and Barbara E. Taylor, *Governance as Leadership: Reframing the Work of Nonprofit Boards* (Hoboken, NJ: John Wiley & Sons, 2005).

disagree, it may be necessary for the board chair to call an individual on disruptive behavior. It is the chair's role, not the chief executive's role, to take the necessary steps for board member discipline. The chair may take an individual aside later for coaching on how to disagree without being disagreeable. Or the chair may explain to a board member why it is poor stewardship to take discord to constituents outside of the boardroom after a board decision has been reached.

One way to promote constructive dissent is to provide well-structured forums for strategic or emerging issues that invite board members to air "dissensus" before the board can arrive at consensus. At one nonprofit organization where the board was deliberating on a potential merger, individual board members were assigned to play roles as ardent opponents or as advocates to help the board thoughtfully consider the pros and cons. Stakeholders were also invited to weigh in on how the merger would positively and negatively affect their relationships with the new organization.

It takes strength of character from both the chair and the chief executive to genuinely invite thoughtful feedback (even when it's critical) from different quarters. It requires grace under pressure for all board members to not penalize individuals who are willing and able to speak truth to power. The American Foreign Service Association (AFSA) is an example of an organization that tries to institutionalize these values.

PETER DRUCKER ON THE DANGERS OF SUPPRESSING DEBATE

- All the first-rate decision makers I've observed had a very simple rule: If you have quick consensus on an important matter, don't make the decision. Acclamation means nobody has done the homework. The organization's decisions are important and risky, and they should be controversial.

- Trust requires that dissent come out in the open. Nonprofit institutions need a healthy atmosphere for dissent if they wish to foster innovation and commitment.

- Without proper encouragement, people have a tendency to avoid such difficult, but vital, discussions or turn them into underground feuds.

- Any organization needs its nonconformist. This is not the kind of person who says, "There is a right way and a wrong way — and our way." Rather, he or she asks, "What is the right way for the future?" and is ready to change. Finally, open discussion uncovers what the objections are. With genuine participation, a decision doesn't need to be sold. Suggestions can be incorporated, objections addressed, and the decision itself becomes a commitment to action

Source: Peter F. Drucker, *The Five Most Important Questions: The Drucker Foundation Self-Assessment Tool for Nonprofit Organizations* (San Francisco: Jossey-Bass Publishers, 1993).

AFSA bestows annual awards on Foreign Service officers for "constructive dissent." These citations are given to individuals who have the courage to challenge the system from within and who "challenge conventional wisdom, intelligently and tenaciously" through appropriate channels. Although it's always hard for someone to go against prevailing wisdom, the State Department believes that international relations benefit from diverse thinking.

Appreciative inquiry (AI), which has been used in strategic planning to invite thoughtful feedback from different stakeholders, provides another mechanism for promoting dialogue and constructive dissent. AI often engages wider participation from stakeholders with a diversity of views to build on what has worked well rather than to fix what seems to be broken. This could be used effectively to draw from board members a vivid picture about what they value currently, where they hope that changes might occur, and how they might get there, by asking board members questions such as:

- What would a successful [outcome of strategic issue or topic] look like to you?

- What has worked really well this year that we can draw lessons from in creating and implementing strategy on [insert strategic issue]? What made it work?

- What are some situations where board or staff members (or other stakeholders) performed exceptionally well in a related area?

- What was fueling such performance?

- What was your best experience of working as part of this board to address a similar issue in a successful manner? What conditions would enable you to continue this experience?

Most boards are uncomfortable in handling situations in which an individual board member chronically attacks others or substitutes disruptive behavior for the concerns that he or she is suppressing. While the board chair will be a key player in reinforcing or undermining the norms for challenging one another's assumptions in a respectful manner, individual board members can foster a culture of inquiry in a number of ways: by reminding the group of its agreed-upon norms of behavior (see chapter 3) and the outcomes of the session, playing back what they are hearing from individuals with contrary views, inviting the group to take a "process check" or time out when needed to allow board members to share perceptions on how well they think the group is deliberating or debating, or simply observing that they are uncomfortable with an exchange or pattern that has violated their group agreements.

Closing Thoughts

"It ain't what you don't know that gets you into trouble. It's what you know for sure that just ain't so." — Mark Twain

Determining how the board can add the greatest value and whether a culture of inquiry will advance the board and the organization should represent strategic choices for nonprofit leaders rather than default practices. Efforts to enhance board effectiveness are not likely to result in significant improvements until key leaders have determined what they most want and need from their board members beyond their obvious fiduciary requirements. This is the real place to start. And a good board self-assessment process that frames questions about the board's genuine role in governance and leadership can ferret out the consensus for and commitment to going forward on this choice.

A culture of inquiry is not a tool or a task, but a style of governing. Is a culture of inquiry something that any board can develop? Yes, but it's impossible to change the culture without the presence of individuals (ideally the chief executive and the board chair) who truly serve as role models and provide the tools for a culture of inquiry. Can a culture of inquiry be maintained once it is established? Yes, but it is an ongoing process, not an intermittent task. Is it worth the effort? The costs of not doing so can be even higher. The absence of a culture of inquiry can lead to groupthink, questionable decisions with unfortunate consequences, and dysfunctional group dynamics. Perhaps the greatest danger is underutilized, bored board members who become passive or disgruntled, or opt out of board service altogether.

Ultimately, a culture of inquiry is a choice that a board makes to be as effective as possible. But the quest for a culture of inquiry may fail unless the board has a road map to help it create, understand, and practice the markers that make such a culture work. While there is no simple formula for building a culture of inquiry, careful moves and measured efforts to deploy the kinds of practices embedded in the four building blocks covered in this book provide a path to this destination.

Learn from Lewis and Clark

Wouldn't the topic of building a nonprofit board make a great new reality show? Imagine this hit show depicting the way changing and diverse members of a key decision-making unit in a major sector of American society learn how to sing or dance together as a high-performing group. Until someone sells that idea, we encourage you to adopt an expeditionary approach. Don't strive for perfection. Governance is not only about vision and strategy. It is also about the process, which is inherently messy because it involves dealing with individual egos, multiple motives, diverse styles, and inevitable conflict. There will be times when your board is enmeshed in an unpredictable situation that will require it to simply muddle though with grace rather than turn to a user's manual.

Do experiment incrementally with some of the tools and methods described in each building block in this book and the sources cited in Suggested Resources. Not every approach will fit every board, and you will find other practices that work with boards you admire. As you pack and unpack your bags to help your board in this continuous learning journey, think about the current culture of your board and the predilections of its members. Determine which approaches might shake them out of their routine tribal rites. Don't be afraid to pack some new tools or discard some old ones for this expedition. Why not start by changing the typical board meeting seating arrangement to host a different group process or by dividing the board into small groups to encourage brainstorming and more airtime on selective issues for shy board members? Above all, try not to let the natural discomfort of change trump widespread dissatisfaction with the status quo. If one hopes to build an exceptional board, one surely needs to start by attracting members with a variety of strengths and abilities. It will be hard to mine this collective wisdom if the board chair, the chief executive, and the collective board do not intentionally support the desired outcome of this journey.

Creating a culture of trust, civility, and inquiry will go a long way toward recruiting and retaining exceptional board members. Talented and able individuals who join a board are not likely to stick around if they find themselves wondering what material difference their presence has really made at each board meeting. Board meetings should not be dismissed as places where "minutes are taken and hours are lost." Only when board members have the tools to make the whole greater than its individual parts can boards become the exceptional source of collective wisdom that they were intended to be. Fostering a culture of inquiry is one important means to ensure that the stellar individuals on your board evolve into an even brighter constellation.

Suggested Resources

Publications

The Source: Twelve Principles of Governance That Power Exceptional Boards.
Washington, DC: BoardSource, 2005. Exceptional boards add significant value to
their organizations, making discernible differences in their advance on mission.
The Source: Twelve Principles of Governance That Power Exceptional Boards defines
governance not as dry, obligatory compliance, but as a creative and collaborative
process that supports chief executives, engages board members, and furthers the
causes they all serve. *The Source* enables nonprofit boards to operate at the highest
and best use of their collective capacity. Aspirational in nature, these principles offer
chief executives a description of an empowered board that is a strategic asset to be
leveraged. They provide board members with a vision of what is possible and a way
to add lasting value to the organizations they lead.

Chait, Richard P., William P. Ryan, and Barbara E. Taylor. *Governance as Leadership:
Reframing the Work of Nonprofit Boards.* Hoboken, NJ: John Wiley & Sons, 2005.
Written by noted consultants and researchers Richard P. Chait, William P. Ryan, and
Barbara E. Taylor, who are attuned to the needs of practitioners, *Governance as
Leadership: Reframing the Work of Nonprofit Boards* redefines nonprofit governance.
It provides a powerful framework for a new covenant between trustees and
executives: more macrogovernance in exchange for less micromanagement.

Flynn, Outi. *Meet Smarter.* Washington, DC: BoardSource, 2004. *Meet Smarter*
provides practical solutions to better meetings by focusing on the process and
practices that will reinvigorate your board meetings. It looks at boards as teams
where group dynamics and communication determine the group's effectiveness.

Katzenbach, Jon R. and Douglas K. Smith. *The Wisdom of Teams: Creating the High-
Performance Organization.* New York: HarperBusiness, 1993. This classic dissects team
behavior, structure, and profile while arguing that we cannot meet the challenges
ahead, from total quality to customer service to innovation, without teams. The
authors talked with hundreds of people in numerous corporate teams to discover
what differentiates various levels of team performance, where and how teams work
best, and how to enhance their effectiveness.

Lencioni, Patrick. *The Five Dysfunctions of a Team.* San Francisco: Jossey-Bass, 2002.
In *The Five Dysfunctions of a Team,* Patrick Lencioni once again offers a leadership
fable that is enthralling and instructive. Throughout the story, Lencioni reveals the
five dysfunctions that go to the very heart of why teams — even the best ones —
often struggle. He outlines a powerful model and actionable steps that can be used
to overcome these common hurdles and build a cohesive, effective team.

Nadler, Gerald and William Chandon. *Smart Questions: Learn to Ask the Right
Questions for Powerful Results.* Hoboken, NJ: John Wiley & Sons, 2004. Based on 40
years of research, *Smart Questions* helps individuals determine the right approach to
understanding their problems. Using this proven approach, readers can move toward
the "good idea" and figure out how to implement it. The principles of successful

problem solving are understood by the smart questions that readers ask to move themselves along in the process. The book shows how anyone can break out of traditional, self-defeating modes of reasoning to find solutions to almost any problem.

Senge, Peter M. *The Fifth Discipline*. New York: Currency and Doubleday, 1990. The objective of *The Fifth Discipline* is to help turn corporations into learning organizations. Senge relies on systems thinking and incorporates into it the other four disciplines: building shared vision, mental models, team learning, and personal mastery.

Surowiecki, James. *The Wisdom of Crowds*. New York: Doubleday/Random House, 2004. Financial journalist James Surowiecki claims that large groups of people are often smarter than an elite few. However, these groups must meet four conditions: diversity, decentralization, independence, and aggregation. In *The Wisdom of Crowds*, Surowiecki explains how collective wisdom shapes business, economies, societies, and nations.

Yankelovich, Daniel. *The Magic of Dialogue: Transforming Conflict into Cooperation*. New York: Simon & Schuster, 1999. Dialogue, when properly practiced, will align people with a shared vision, and help them realize their full potential as individuals and as a team. Drawing on decades of research and using real life examples, *The Magic of Dialogue* outlines specific strategies for maneuvering in a wide range of situations and teaches managers, leaders, business people, and other professionals how to succeed in the new global economy, where more players participate in decision making than ever before.

ARTICLES

Axelrod, Nancy R. "In the Boardroom, Culture Counts." *Journal of Association Leadership*, Fall 2004. Board culture has a great impact on the quality of decisions boards make. Nancy Axelrod explains that board cultures that promote trust, teamwork, candor, and constructive conflict influence the board's performance. She guides chief executives and chairs to become "chief board development officers."

Axelrod, Nancy R., Scott Cowen, Harvey P. Dale, Martin Michaelson, Barry Munitz, and Sheldon Steinbach. "Don't Be Known as Enron U." *Trusteeship*, July/August 2002. Five experts on higher education question what kind of an impact the Enron debacle might have on colleges or universities.

Bazerman, Max and Dolly Chugh. "Decisions Without Blinders." *Harvard Business Review*, January 2006. "Bounded awareness" occurs during different phases of decision making and prevents an organization or an individual from profiting from all the information available. Four obstacles contribute to this phenomenon: failure to see information, failure to seek information, failure to use information, and failure to share information.

Charan, Ram. "Conquering a Culture of Indecision." *Harvard Business Review*, April 2001. Lack of adequate communication tends to be the main culprit when the chief executive's decisions and directives go ignored. Charan recommends "decisive dialogues" to guide staff. These dialogues have four components: They must include a sincere search for answers, tolerate unpleasant truths, invite a full range of views, and provide clear steps for action.

Robinson, Maureen. "Declaration of Independence." *Board Member*, March/April 2007. In this article, Maureen Robinson discusses independent-mindedness, unbiased and conflict-of-interest–free decision making in the boardroom. She stresses the importance of positive neutrality as a tool to help the board step back and provide a deliberately neutral perspective on an issue under discussion.

Tuckman, Bruce. "Developmental Sequence in Small Groups." *Psychological Bulletin*, 63, 1965. Decades ago Tuckman introduced his theory on the phases that are inevitable and necessary for a team to grow, face new challenges, and find solutions. His Forming-Storming-Norming-Performing model has evolved into a widely used management theory on group dynamics and how teams function.

About the Author

Nancy R. Axelrod, principal of NonProfit Leadership Services, is an independent consultant who provides services to nonprofit organizations in board education, development, self-assessment, and leadership transitions. She has served as a governing and advisory board member and board development consultant to numerous associations, foundations, charitable organizations, higher education institutions, and other nonprofit organizations. She is a member of the faculty of both the Institute for Board Chairs and Presidents of Independent Colleges and Universities sponsored by the Association of Governing Boards of Universities and Colleges, and the Center for Association Leadership, a national learning center and think tank in Washington, D.C.

Nancy is the founding president of the National Center for Nonprofit Boards (now known as BoardSource), where she served as the chief executive officer from 1987 – 1996. In addition to providing board development services to a variety of nonprofit organizations, she frequently serves as a speaker at forums dedicated to governance and accountability. She is the author of *Chief Executive Succession Planning: The Board's Role in Securing Your Organization's Future*; *Advisory Councils*; a contributing author to *The Jossey-Bass Handbook of Nonprofit Leadership and Management*; and has written numerous articles and op-ed pieces. Nancy currently serves as a member of the Advisory Board of the Initiative on Social Enterprise at the Harvard Business School and the Review Panel of the NACD Not-For-Profit Director of the Year Award. She is a former chairman of the Board of Trustees of the Association Leadership Foundation of the Greater Washington Society of Association Executives.

Nancy can be reached at naxelrod@rcn.com.